CONSUMING PASSIONS

A Play in Two Parts

by Alan Ayckbourn

FOR AMATEUR PRODUCTION ENQUIRIES

UNITED KINGDOM AND WORLD
EXCLUDING NORTH AMERICA
licensing@concordtheatricals.co.uk
020-7054-7200

Each title is subject to availability from Concord Theatricals,
depending upon country of performance.

MUSIC USE NOTE

Licensees are solely responsible for obtaining formal written permission from copyright owners to use copyrighted music in the performance of this play and are strongly cautioned to do so. If no such permission is obtained by the licensee, then the licensee must use only original music that the licensee owns and controls. Licensees are solely responsible and liable for all music clearances and shall indemnify the copyright owners of the play(s) and their licensing agent, Concord Theatricals, against any costs, expenses, losses and liabilities arising from the use of music by licensees. Please contact the appropriate music licensing authority in your territory for the rights to any incidental music.

USE OF COPYRIGHT MUSIC

A licence issued by Samuel French Ltd to perform this play does not include permission to use the incidental music specified in this copy. Where the place of performance is already licensed by the PERFORMING RIGHT SOCIETY (PRS) a return of the music used must be made to them. If the place of performance is not so licensed then application should be made to the PRS, 2 Pancras Square, London, N1C 4AG (www.prsformusic.com). A separate and additional licence from PHONOGRAPHIC PERFORMANCE LTD, 1 Upper James Street, London W1F 9DE (www.ppluk.com) is needed whenever commercial recordings are used.

IMPORTANT BILLING AND CREDIT REQUIREMENTS

If you have obtained performance rights to this title, please refer to your licensing agreement for important billing and credit requirements.

CONSUMING PASSIONS

First performed at the Stephen Joseph Theatre, Scarborough, in the McCarthy auditorium on 12 August 2016, with the following cast:

CORA / FEMALE PC	Rachel Caffrey
FREDDY / EDMUND / PC	Andy Cryer
MELANIE	Louise Shuttleworth
AGGI / DINKA / CEDRIC	Leigh Symonds

Director Alan Ayckbourn
Designer Kevin Jenkins

PREMONITIONS

CHARACTERS

MELANIE
CORA
FREDDY

AGGI*
DINKA*

*Played by the same actor

TIME

One Monday/Tuesday evening.

SETTING

Ristorante Calvinu, a bistro.

Ristorante Calvinu, a popular, low-priced, informal bistro of no fixed nationality.

A table, in a remote alcove, currently laid for four. Chargers, basic glassware, but no cutlery as yet.

Despite being a Monday, in the background at another table nearby, a rowdy party is celebrating.

DINKA, a rather sullen waiter, leads on MELANIE, a woman in her forties.

DINKA *(somewhat ungraciously)* Here you are.

MELANIE Thank you.

DINKA This quiet enough for you?

MELANIE Thank you, this will do nicely. That other table was right on top of that rowdy party, that's all. I couldn't have heard myself think.

DINKA That's Mr Miller. That's his party. They're celebrating.

MELANIE They certainly were...

DINKA Mr Miller, he's a good customer. He comes here a lot to celebrate.

MELANIE What are they celebrating?

DINKA I don't know. Birthday. Anniversary. Engagement. I don't know. I don't ask. Mr Miller and his family, they always celebrating something. Celebratory family, eh?

MELANIE Well, I wish they'd do it more quietly...

DINKA He's a good customer. This table's just for you?

MELANIE No, I said, I'm expecting someone else to join me. He's going to be a trifle late.

DINKA Oh, yes? Your husband, again, eh?

MELANIE *(guardedly)* Possibly...

DINKA I remember from the other day. He was late that time.

MELANIE Yes, well, he's a very busy man...

DINKA You sit here for two hours waiting for him and he don't show. Nothing all evening except one jug of tap water, he never show –

MELANIE It was an important meeting –

DINKA – what kind of husband leave his wife all evening with just a jug of tap water...?

MELANIE – he couldn't get in touch with me, the meeting overran. As I say, he's a very busy man. Extremely busy...

DINKA He don't turn up for you tonight, I tell you, you divorce him – that's what I'd do...

MELANIE That's what you'd do, is it?

DINKA What?

MELANIE Divorce your wife?

DINKA Me? I don't have a wife. I got more sense. You want a drink while you wait for him?

MELANIE No. I'd just like a jug of water, please.

DINKA Water?

MELANIE A jug of tap water.

DINKA Tap water?

MELANIE Yes, please.

DINKA All right but in an hour, this table is needed.

MELANIE Needed?

DINKA It's booked for somebody else. You ring him, tell him if he don't get here soon, he won't get no dinner.

MELANIE Oh, really that's outrageous...

DINKA It's already booked for someone else. Someone who wants to eat.

MELANIE Well, I'm certainly not moving! I've booked this table for the evening –

DINKA I get your jug of tap water...

He moves away.

MELANIE *(calling after him)* – we're certainly not moving, we refuse to – *(alone)* Charmless man. Absolutely graceless. The last time we eat here. The very last time.

She sits and looks about her. A loud burst of merriment from the offstage party.

(not quite loud enough to be heard) Oh, do shut up, shut up, shut up! Rowdy lot! Celebrate more quietly, can't you? Have some consideration for others!

She takes out her mobile phone and places it on the table. She looks at her watch.

Well, if you stand me up again tonight, John, I think we really will be looking at a divorce. Enough is enough, my darling.

Another loud burst of merriment.

She glares across at them. Someone evidently sees her and reacts. She pulls a face back at them.

AGGI, *another waiter, enters. As he does so, the restaurant ambience grows suddenly much quieter, as if it is suddenly a different night, possibly the following night, Tuesday.* AGGI *looks somewhat similar to his colleague but is of a much sunnier disposition.*

Following him is CORA, *in her thirties. She is wearing a headscarf and dark glasses in an attempt at anonymity.*

AGGI *shows her to the table.*

AGGI Here we are, this table here. Nice and quiet, for you. You won't be disturbed, here.

He seats CORA.

MELANIE *looks on indignantly.*

They both seem totally unaware of her.

CORA Thank you.

MELANIE *(recovering, much affronted)* I say, excuse me! Do you mind?

AGGI Would you like a drink, madametta, while you wait for him?

CORA Yes, I'll have a large gin and tonic, thank you. Bombay Sapphire, if you have it...

MELANIE I say –

AGGI Bombay Sapphire. Tonic. Slimline, yes?

CORA Slimline, yes please.

MELANIE Look, I'm sorry, this table is reserved! Do you mind most awfully?

AGGI *(departing)* Right away!

MELANIE *(calling after him)* Waiter, that seat is taken! There's going to be someone sitting there in a minute...

AGGI *has gone.* MELANIE *glares at* CORA, *who still seems totally unaware of her.*

(to CORA*)* You can't sit there, you know. My husband's going to be joining me any minute. He's going to need that seat. I'm terribly sorry, this is a reserved table. You can't just sit there, you know.

CORA, *ignoring her, delves into her handbag and locates her phone, which she starts to check for messages.*

Oh, yes, you can ignore me as much as you like but the point is, I was here first. I'm calling the waiter and I'm going to ask him to move you. Do you hear me?

CORA *reads a message on her screen that causes her to smile.*

It may be a big joke to you, madam, but let me tell you, I don't find this funny, not at all. Calmly sitting down at someone else's –

DINKA *has returned from the other direction with a jug of iced tap water.*

Ah, waiter... Would you kindly tell this woman, I don't know who on earth she is –

DINKA *(plonking down the jug)* Tap water!

MELANIE – will you tell her to move at once! Go on, tell her!

DINKA *looks puzzled.*

Go on! She doesn't take a blind bit of notice of me! Tell her!

DINKA Tell who?

MELANIE This woman! Tell her to move, this is my table!

DINKA What woman?

MELANIE That woman, there!

DINKA I don't see no woman. *(moving off)* Enjoy your tap water!

MELANIE *(calling after him)* Will you tell her at once kindly not to sit at my table!

But DINKA has gone.

CORA *is still playing with her phone, oblivious to all this.*

MELANIE *fumes.*

My husband will be joining me in a moment you know. He's due any minute. Any moment now. Then you'll have to move, won't you? He'll make you move. He's a very high-powered man. Very important. He'll get you to move, see if he doesn't! He's a former rugger blue. He won't stand any nonsense, I can tell you.

CORA *obliviously continues with her phone.*

(frustratedly) Listen, don't keep ignoring me! Will you have the common courtesy to look at me, please!

AGGI *returns, carrying a tray with* CORA'*s drink. He is with* FREDDY, *who is in his late twenties wearing a distinctive cap pulled down, half concealing his face.*

AGGI Here he is! He's here!

FREDDY *(to* CORA*)* At last! At last! Darling, I'm so sorry!

CORA Darling! Where on earth have you been, you idiot?

They embrace.

MELANIE Oh, now this is just too much! What on earth is going on here? Really! Waiter, will you please stop showing people to my table!

FREDDY Sorry, got on the wrong tube...went halfway to Tooting...

CORA Yes, I just got your message...

AGGI *(delivering the drink)* One Bombay Sapphire –

FREDDY Hey! Look at you! Hardly recognised you –

MELANIE Excuse me, waiter!

AGGI – one slimline tonic.

CORA *(to* AGGI*)* Thank you. *(to* FREDDY*)* Just in case someone recognised me, we can't be too careful. Even out here.

FREDDY Bet you didn't recognise me, did you? –

CORA I'd recognise you anywhere, you clown!

MELANIE *(indignantly)* Listen, you two, excuse me! I am here you know! I am sitting here!

CORA That ridiculous hat! Take it off, you idiot!

MELANIE *(loudly)* I say, excuse me, you two!

FREDDY *(removing it)* Don't you like it, I think it rather suits me –

MELANIE Waiter, I want it known, this is the very last time I am setting foot in this restaurant –

AGGI May I take your hat, sir?

MELANIE – ever again –

FREDDY *(handing it to* AGGI*)* Thanks.

CORA Yes, please do. Take it away.

MELANIE – the very last time –

FREDDY You said incognito.

MELANIE – ever!

CORA I said unobtrusive.

FREDDY Same thing. Unobtrusive – incognito.

MELANIE Is that clear?

AGGI Can I get you a drink, sir?

FREDDY Scotch and soda, thanks very much. *(to* CORA*)* Incognito.

AGGI One Scotch-soda, coming up!

He goes off.

CORA No, not incognito, unobtrusive –

MELANIE I'm sorry, I am not sitting here a minute longer –

CORA – meaning do not wear something that makes you stand out a mile!

MELANIE *(rising)* – I am moving to another table.

She stands up and looks around her rather aimlessly, clutching her glass and the water jug, searching round for a vacant table.

FREDDY and **CORA** *continue, obliviously unaware of her.*

FREDDY Where the hell are we, anyway? What is this place?

CORA It's known as South of the River, darling. No need to panic you're perfectly safe. *(taking his hand across the table)* It's good to see you. I've missed you.

FREDDY Same here. Missed you, too. God knows, I've missed you, my darling.

CORA Won't be much longer –

FREDDY *(uncertainly)* Yes...

CORA We must be strong! We can do it! Together.

They gaze intently into each other's eyes.

DINKA *returns from the other direction, on his way to somewhere else with a tray. He stops as he sees* **MELANIE***.*

DINKA *(to* **MELANIE***, suspiciously)* What you doing? Where you going?

MELANIE Ah, waiter! You are my waiter, aren't you –?

DINKA You leaving?

MELANIE – you all look so terribly alike.

DINKA You going, you leave the jug there –

MELANIE Now, listen to me, your colleague, without so much as a by-your-leave, has just shown these people to my table –

DINKA – that jug the property of the management. You can't take that away –

MELANIE – now either they leave, or show me to another table – are you listening to me, waiter –?

DINKA – you put the jug down, you hear? You can't take the jug –

MELANIE *(banging the jug down on the table)* I don't want your wretched jug! I simply want these people moved!

DINKA What people?

MELANIE These two people here! This person – and this – other – person! Both of them! I want them both to move!

DINKA *stares at her for a second.*

DINKA You're crazy.

MELANIE I beg your pardon?

DINKA You see people?

MELANIE Of course I can see them.

DINKA Sitting there?

MELANIE Yes!

DINKA Two people?

MELANIE Yes! A man – here! And a woman – here!

DINKA You're crazy.

MELANIE How dare you?

DINKA I don't see no one. There's no one.

MELANIE But they were being served by the other waiter. Your colleague.

DINKA Other waiter? What other waiter?

MELANIE He was – I can't see him at the moment – he looks very much like you – about your height, maybe a little taller. And I think he has a moustache.

DINKA Moustache? Waiter with a moustache?

MELANIE I'm almost sure he has –

DINKA That's my brother.

MELANIE Ah, there you are then! Now, do you believe me?

DINKA No, I don't believe you.

MELANIE Why not?

DINKA He's not working tonight.

MELANIE But I've just this minute seen him.

DINKA My brother, he don't work Mondays. His night off.

MELANIE Well, he's certainly here now. I saw him.

DINKA Tonight, he's at the football. He's not here. Now you want to leave, you want to stay, make up your mind. I got other people to look after –

MELANIE Well, could I – possibly – I demand another table, please. A table on my own.

DINKA There's no other tables, we're full. You sit there. Don't take the jug.

He goes off.

MELANIE *sits again. She is getting slightly hysterical.*
CORA *and* FREDDY *are still locked together, hands held.*

MELANIE *(to the others, with a laugh)* Did you hear that just now? Did you ever hear anything like it? He claims he can't even see you...ridiculous. It's like you were invisible! Absurd. You almost feel like laughing...don't you? Really?

The couple still don't acknowledge her.

I mean, I can see you. Perfectly clearly. Idiotic man!

AGGI *returns with a glass of Scotch and a soda water bottle on a tray.*

Ah now, the very person. Waiter, I've just been speaking to your brother and he tells me...

AGGI *(putting them down, ignoring her)* One Scotch and soda. Thank you, sirrah.

FREDDY *(absently)* Thanks...

MELANIE He told me you weren't working here tonight but that is palpably untrue isn't it? Your brother was clearly lying to me... *(tailing off)* ...wasn't he?

AGGI *has gone without so much as glancing at her.*
MELANIE *is starting to panic slightly.*

What on earth's the matter with these people? He took absolutely no notice of me. Like I didn't even exist... You can see me. Can't you? You two? You can see me? Can't you?

FREDDY *(to* CORA*)* Cheers!

CORA To us.

They toast.

MELANIE I can see you, you know...

FREDDY God, you're sexy. Even dressed like that. Especially dressed like that. Like some bloody Mata Hari. I want to make love to you right now...

CORA Oh, God, yes... Yes, please.

FREDDY Right here and now. I'll spread you across this bloody table...

CORA *(getting excited)* Oh, please...

MELANIE Oh, my God – this is simply too much –

She snatches up her water jug.

FREDDY Come on, then! What about it, baby?

CORA No, we can't, darling – not now –

FREDDY Come on, get 'em off...

CORA – we really can't, not here –

MELANIE No, you certainly can't...

FREDDY Come on, let's get out of this place, then...

MELANIE Please, do –

FREDDY – we'll go somewhere else...

MELANIE – the sooner the better!

CORA Where else is there? Where the hell can we go, darling?
Be practical.

FREDDY Some hotel, some knocking shop... I don't care... I can't
take much more of this –

MELANIE Neither can I!

FREDDY – I don't care about the risks. Let him find out! See
if I care! I don't care if he does...

CORA *(calming him)* Darling, my sweet darling, you're so young
and impetuous, aren't you? It'll all be over soon, I promise.
Be patient just for a little bit longer. We've waited this long –

FREDDY This waiting! It's agony! I need you so much...

CORA – only another week, sweetheart. Listen, today's Tuesday –
one more week, that's all –

MELANIE No, it's not, it's Monday –

CORA One more week –

MELANIE Today's Monday –

CORA Just think of that. One more week –

MELANIE You didn't think this was Tuesday, did you?

CORA – and it'll finally all be over.

MELANIE Oh, that's what it is. That's the confusion. You're here
on the wrong night!

CORA In exactly one week's time, next Tuesday –

MELANIE Next Monday –

CORA – it'll be our tenth wedding anniversary –

FREDDY I can't believe you've been married to that bastard
for that long –

CORA No, listen, I know what he's like. He gets so sentimental
about these things. Next Tuesday we'll be having dinner
out as usual with friends –

MELANIE No, next Monday –

FREDDY You're not eating in this place, I trust –

MELANIE – in a week's time it will be Monday –

CORA God no! He wouldn't be seen dead in a place like this – Can you imagine him –? No, we'll be dining somewhere terribly smart and stuffy – with one or two friends – mostly his friends – I scarcely have any friends of my own, these days –

MELANIE I'm hardly surprised –

FREDDY Apart from me –

CORA Apart from you, of course, my darling. Then when that's over – he and I, we plan to drive to the cottage – or rather I'll drive – he'll certainly be well away by then, I'll make sure of that. And once we're there, just before midnight, I'll suggest to him that what would really make the evening really complete would be for us to renew our vows together – privately in secret – just the two of us – and I'll suggest the perfect spot for it – the very place where he first proposed all those years ago – up on Craghead Rock – just a ten-minute walk away – one of the reasons he bought that wretched little cottage in the first place – the view is spectacular up there, on a good day, they say, you can see four counties –

FREDDY Not in the middle of the night, you can't, surely?

CORA Yes, midnight. But we won't be looking at the view darling – we'll be doing what we did on that night we first got engaged – first he knelt down and proposed to me, all very proper and traditional like he always is. And then after that I'll kneel in front of him – all very improper and untraditional –

FREDDY I can't bear to think of that! You and him –

MELANIE Oh, I'm beginning not to like the sound of this, either –

CORA Just to keep his mind occupied so he doesn't see you till the very last minute –

FREDDY Where will I be?

CORA There's some thick shrubbery just a yard or so in from the edge of the cliff –

MELANIE – not one little bit...

CORA I checked it's still there, last weekend. It's the perfect spot. Don't worry, he won't see you till the last minute. I'll make sure he's very close to the edge – just a tiny nudge – that's all it'll take –

FREDDY Just a little push...?

CORA I promise he'll never know till the very last minute. At least the bastard'll die with a smile on his face –

MELANIE Oh, you minx, you little minx! On the poor man's wedding anniversary! Have you no shame?

CORA And then we'll be together for ever my darling...

FREDDY For ever and ever?

CORA For ever and ever.

FREDDY Until death us do part?

MELANIE Until she decides to push you off a cliff as well, you stupid man.

FREDDY God! It sounds so simple doesn't it? So what time do you want me up there, in the bushes?

CORA Well shall we say, half eleven – just to be on the safe side.

FREDDY Just wondering which car to use. Not the Alfa, not on that cart track. Wreck the suspension. Sounds like a job for the SUV.

CORA Yes, whatever. Nothing too ostentatious. Just so long as you don't bring that ghastly yellow thing.

FREDDY God, no. Not the Alfa. Not halfway up a mountain. *(thoughtfully)* Yes...

CORA What's the matter? You're not having doubts, are you?

MELANIE Please, please, have doubts... Please!

FREDDY I was just thinking. Half an hour crouching in some bushes on the top of a cliff –?

CORA All right, twenty minutes, then, make it twenty minutes –

FREDDY And then I was thinking, what if it's raining?

MELANIE Exactly.

CORA It won't rain. I've checked the forecast – five per cent probability –

FREDDY What if someone else is up there?

MELANIE Yes! What then?

CORA At midnight? Who the hell else is going to be up there at that time in that godforsaken spot?

FREDDY Well maybe they've gone up there to look at the – oh, yes, I see what you mean. *(slight pause)* I don't know, you know. I'm not sure, now. I can't – I can't quite see myself as someone who pushes somebody else off a cliff, I really can't. I'm sorry. It seems a bit – heartless...

CORA *(wheedling)* For me? Just a weeny push? A teeny-weeny push? You've said it yourself, it's so simple. Wouldn't you do that? For me? I do so love you, Freddy. I so badly want to share the rest of my life with you, darling. Don't you want that, as well? Don't you?

MELANIE No! Say no, you idiot! Say no –

FREDDY Well...

MELANIE – can't you see she's just using you? Toying with you, you oaf!

CORA I love you so much. So, so much...

FREDDY Yes, I know. *(slight pause)* Listen, you aren't just saying that, are you?

CORA What?

MELANIE Of course she is, the harpy. She's just saying that!

FREDDY You're not just saying that in order to make me –? So you can get shot of him, are you? And then plan to simply ditch me afterwards?

MELANIE Ah, a little bit of sense, at last!

CORA You think I'd do that? You really think I'm like that, Freddy? You think I'd really stoop as low as that?

MELANIE Yes!

FREDDY Well. It did cross my mind. I mean, don't take it the wrong –

CORA *(suddenly cooling, abruptly)* All right! If that's what you think of me, Freddy, forget it! Forget the whole thing!

FREDDY Oh, come on, be fair –

MELANIE Don't weaken now!

CORA Forget it, then. Forget us, forget me – forget everything!

FREDDY Forget us? Just like that?

CORA I thought I could rely on you, Freddy. I stupidly depended on you, you know. If you don't care about me, about my happiness, if you want me to stay trapped like a prisoner inside a miserable, loveless marriage – Oh, God, I'm such a fool, aren't I? Such a fool? Such a simple-minded, trusting fool?

FREDDY *(ineffectually)* Not at all...

CORA I blame myself. I'm a silly little romantic pathetic female with her head in the clouds, who actually believed her white knight had finally arrived to rescue her. What a fool!

MELANIE Oh, God hark at her!

FREDDY *(bemused)* Hang on a tick, I think you're being a bit unfair here – all I said was –

CORA I know what you said! I know what you said! Forget the whole thing, Freddy, it's over! Fini! Kaput! Curtain!

FREDDY Cora!

CORA Finale! Close! Dissolve! All right, let's shed the disguises and pretences shall we? Pretend this was ever going to happen? Let's face it, it's never going to happen, is it?

She rises and takes off her headscarf and dark glasses, rather melodramatically.

FREDDY *(miserably)* Oh, Lord...all I said was...

MELANIE *(staring at* CORA, *with a growing realisation)* Oh, my God! It can't be! It's her! Her! Mrs Collison! It's Mrs Collison... Oh, goodness! Oh for heaven's sake! Oh, how terrible! Now what do I do? What on earth am I going to do?

FREDDY Where are you going?

CORA Goodbye, Freddy. It was great fun while it lasted. I had hoped for something deeper, more permanent. But then, who am I to hope? I probably don't deserve happiness anyway.

She turns tearfully to go. AGGI *arrives.*

AGGI Madametta, you're leaving?

CORA Yes, I'm sorry, I have to go.

AGGI Everything all right for you?

CORA Thank you, very nice. You don't mind if I leave you with the bill, Freddy? *(choking back her tears)* I think the least you can do is to buy me a drink, don't you?

FREDDY *(rather stunned)* Sure.

CORA *goes out.*

AGGI Goodnight, madametta, have a good evening! Sirrah? Can I get you something else? Something to eat?

FREDDY No, thanks. Not that hungry. *(indicating his drink)* Get me another one of these, though, if you don't mind.

AGGI One more Scotch-soda.

FREDDY And I'll have the bill at the same time, please.

AGGI Not eating? No? Certainly.

He goes out.

FREDDY *(gloomily)* Oh, Lord...

MELANIE I know you can't hear me, but well done, young man. Well done!

FREDDY Now what?

MELANIE Let me tell you, you are well out of that. That woman is not to be trusted. I've known all along she was a shallow little gold-digger. She married Cedric – Mr Collison – when the poor man – He was still mourning the loss of his first wife, Anthea – who was, in all honesty, I have to say it, a saint – She was barely cold in her grave – the rest of us in the office, we loyally stood by Cedric – supporting him – keeping a respectful distance, allowing him proper time to grieve – not wishing to crowd him in any way – giving him space to – recover – to heal.

AGGI *returns with another Scotch and soda for* **FREDDY**, *plus the bill in a folder. He puts it down and departs.* **FREDDY** *nods a silent acknowledgement.*

And then what happens. You leapt straight in didn't you, Cora Higgins, and you took flagrant advantage of him, didn't you? Ruthlessly sensing Cedric's vulnerability. Whilst the rest of us stood hopelessly by – she brought that noble, caring, gifted, loving, perfect man – that paragon – to his knees with her vulgar little displays of sexual exhibitionism, her barefaced lurid conniving... Yes, we all had your number, Cora Higgins, I can tell you – Yes, you're well clear of that one, young man. That was a very narrow escape for you, I can tell you.

DINKA *has arrived and watches her. He shakes his head.*

DINKA He's not arrived yet?

MELANIE Who?

DINKA Your husband? Still not here?

MELANIE No, palpably not.

DINKA He's not here soon we need this table. We full tonight we need the table.

MELANIE He'll be here in a moment.

DINKA You say that half an hour ago.

MELANIE If you must know, there will now be four of us.

DINKA Four?

MELANIE I'm expecting three others. My husband, John is meeting my son, David, at Paddington who is on his way down from Oxford. That's Oxford University. Where he's reading Law, Physics and Social Psychology. My son, David, is travelling down with his fiancée, Sally, who's an arts graduate and a middle-distance athlete. They'll all be joining me for dinner so we'll be needing this table. And put lots of champagne on ice, please, because we're going to be celebrating.

DINKA *(a bit impressed)* Ice. Right. What you celebrating?

MELANIE Our wedding anniversary. It's our tenth wedding anniversary.

DINKA Congratulations. You want to order a drink, then? A proper drink?

MELANIE No, I'll wait for them. Just have the champagne ready. You can bring me some fresh water, though. *(handing him the jug)* Here. The same again.

DINKA *(darkening again)* More water? You have much more of this, I'm going to start charging.

MELANIE That's outrageous. It's just tap water. It's free isn't it?

DINKA Maybe. But it's out of our tap.

He goes off with the jug.

FREDDY *is still sitting, staring into space. He now has his mobile phone, which he is tossing from hand to hand.*

MELANIE *(regarding him)* Poor boy. Poor boy...

FREDDY *comes to a decision. He opens his phone and speed-dials a number.*

Oh, dear, no...no...

FREDDY *gets through to an answering service.*

FREDDY *(into phone)* Hallo, darling it's me. I hope you pick this up, sometime. Listen, I'm so sorry. So terribly sorry. I've behaved appallingly, just now. I feel I've let you down in every way.

MELANIE No, no, no... You silly boy...

FREDDY ...Can you ever forgive me? I want to make it up to you, Cora. Listen, I'll be there a week from today, Craghead Rock. I promise. At midnight. In the bushes. I'll be waiting for you, darling...

MELANIE Oh, no, no, you mustn't! You mustn't let her get away with it! Stop that at once! Stop it!

She grabs vainly at his phone to snatch it from him but appears to grasp thin air.

FREDDY *(unaware of this)* Don't worry, your white knight is coming, baby. He's up and mounted and on his way!

He downs the second Scotch, grabs up his bill and goes off.

MELANIE Someone, stop him! This man has to be stopped! This has to be prevented! Someone has got to stop it! *(shouting loudly)* If there's anyone here who can possibly hear me or see me! Please! Please! Listen to me! Please listen! *(loudly)* WILL YOU LISTEN!!

There is sudden silence in the restaurant.

DINKA *reappears with the refreshed water jug.*

DINKA Hey! Hey! Hey! What you doing?

MELANIE Everybody! This is most terribly important! In exactly one week's time, next Monday, no, next Tuesday at midnight at Craghead Rock which is somewhere in Dorset. I think. No, Wiltshire. It's in Wiltshire. A man is going to be murdered. Only it won't look like murder, it'll appear to be an accident, only it won't be –

DINKA *puts down the tray and moves to her.*

While the poor man's wicked wife is – is pleasuring him, her lover is going to push him over the edge...and they're going to pass it off as an accident. His name is Cedric Collison, he's the managing director of Brownlow and Johnson who are investment consultants with whom I used to work as Mr Collison's personal assistant until I was forced to retire, purely for health reasons...

DINKA *(over this last)* Come on, you! Out, out out! That's enough! *(grasping her elbow)* Out you go! I give you fair warning. Out you go!

MELANIE Will you let go of me! You have to listen. Please! Please, listen to me!

MELANIE, *protesting and struggling, is propelled by* DINKA *out of the restaurant.*

(her cries, receding, off) Please! Please! Please! You have to listen to me!

She is cut off sharply as the offstage street door closes on her.

DINKA *returns.*

DINKA Sorry, folks, crazy lady. She's a crazy lady. Take no notice. Enjoy yourselves! Eat up! Benzay appertass!

As he picks up the discarded water jug, shaking his head, the restaurant chatter resumes once more.

Blackout.

REPERCUSSIONS

CHARACTERS

MELANIE
CEDRIC
CORA**

EDMUND*
POLICE SERGEANT*
FEMALE PC**

*Played by the same actor
**Played by the same actor

TIME

The next Tuesday evening.

SETTING

The bar area of Mayhew's, a smart restaurant.

*A quiet corner of the bar/pre-drinks area of Mayhew's,
an exclusive London restaurant. Two entrances, one to
the bar and street, the other to the restaurant.*

*A table for four with coasters and a fancy cocktail menu.
Soft piano music.**

EDMUND, *a smart waiter, leads in* **CEDRIC,** *a businessman.*

EDMUND Would you care to sit at your dining table or would you
prefer to wait for your guests, here in the bar, Mr Collison?

CEDRIC No, I'll wait out here till they arrive. I'm a trifle early.
Came straight from work.

EDMUND Would you care for a drink while you're waiting, sir?

CEDRIC Yes, I'll have my usual, Edmund. Vodka martini –

EDMUND – *(swiftly)* Vodka martini – stirred with ice –

CEDRIC – with ice, twist of lemon –

EDMUND – and no olive... Right away, sir.

He goes off to the bar.

CEDRIC Thank you, so much.

He sits at the table.

He looks around him.

He takes out his phone and checks for messages.

EDMUND *returns with a bowl of nuts.*

---

*A licence to produce *Consuming Passions* does not include a performance
licence for any third-party or copyrighted music. Licensees should create an
original composition or use music in the public domain. For further information,
please see Music Use Note on page iii.

EDMUND Just leave those there for you, sir.

CEDRIC *(without looking up)* Oh, by the way, Edmund, I did
ask the restaurant, as soon as everyone's here to open up a
bottle or two of decent champagne –

EDMUND I'll just check they've remembered, sir.

CEDRIC Tell them, not their house stuff, something drinkable –

EDMUND *(as he goes off)* I'll see to that, sir.

He goes off to the restaurant.

CEDRIC *continues to study his phone.*

*He sees the bowl of nuts. He pulls it closer and examines
the contents with a degree of suspicion. He stirs them
with his finger.*

EDMUND *returns.*

That's all taken care of, sir. I've advised the wine waiter.

CEDRIC *(still studying the nuts)* Thank you.

EDMUND Special occasion, is it, sir?

CEDRIC What?

EDMUND This evening. Are you celebrating a special occasion?

CEDRIC Oh, nothing that special. Just a wedding anniversary.
My wife rather – she rather goes in for these sort of things,
you know...

EDMUND Oh, really? May I ask how long it's been, sir?

CEDRIC God knows! About ten years, I think.

EDMUND Ten years! Congratulations, sir.

CEDRIC *(muttering half to himself)* I think it's ten years...must
be all of that... Eleven years since Anthea died... Do you
remember Anthea, Edmund? My first wife? Remember her,
do you? We used to come in here a lot in the old days...

EDMUND I'm afraid before my time, sir. Just to confirm, there will be just the six of you, will there?

CEDRIC What?

EDMUND Just the six of you dining with us tonight?

CEDRIC Yes, just six. So far as I know. Unless she's invited someone else.

EDMUND *(looking off to the bar)* Ah! Your drink, sir. Just one moment.

He goes off swiftly to the bar and returns immediately with CEDRIC's *drink.* CEDRIC *resumes his study of the nuts.*

One vodka martini, with ice, strained with a twist of lemon, no olive.

CEDRIC Edmund, what the hell are these things in here?

EDMUND *(examining the bowl)* Those, sir?

CEDRIC Any idea what they're meant to be?

EDMUND I think they're meant to be nuts, sir.

CEDRIC What on earth are they covered in?

EDMUND *(unsure)* I think it might be some sort of flavouring, possibly. Some type of spice perhaps.

CEDRIC Well, take them away and bring me some proper nuts, plain ones.

EDMUND You prefer plain nuts, sir?

CEDRIC The plainer the better. I don't know where on earth those come from. Certainly don't grow on any tree I've heard of.

EDMUND *removes the bowl.*

EDMUND Can I get you anything else instead, sir? Some crisps?

CEDRIC Yes, bring us a bag of crisps, why not? Let's live it up!

EDMUND *goes off to the bar.*

CEDRIC *sips his drink.*

CEDRIC Ah! That's good. That's very good.

EDMUND *returns from the bar.*

EDMUND Now, it appears we do have a wide choice of crisps, sir. We have smoked cheese and bacon. Cheddar cheese and onion. Worcester sauce and sundried tomato. Tomato, basil and mozzarella. Sweet chilli chicken. Beef and onion. Spicy prawn cocktail. Or apparently the very latest, prosecco and elderflower –

CEDRIC Oh for the love of God! Just a bag of plain crisps, Edmund! Crisps, man!

EDMUND *(as he leaves)* I'll see if we have some plain ones, sir. Oh, by the way, the nuts are apparently coated in sweet chilli potato and maize flour...

He goes off to the bar.

CEDRIC *(muttering)* For God's sake! Prosecco and elderflower... What next? Prune and cucumber? Sardine and artichoke? Claret and coriander?

EDMUND *returns from the bar.*

EDMUND *(confidentially)* Excuse me, sir. Your personal assistant is outside.

CEDRIC My personal assis–? Who, Mary? Good God, what's she doing here at this hour? I thought she'd gone home ages ago. What's she want?

EDMUND She says she's sorry to disturb you, Mr Collison, but it's a matter of some urgency – some important signature, she overlooked, apparently.

CEDRIC Really? How very odd. Can't recall I needed to – Oh, well, let her in, Edmund – This'd better be quick.

EDMUND *(as he goes)* I wouldn't normally disturb you, but it did seem quite urgent.

He goes back in the direction of the bar. CEDRIC *is puzzled.*

CEDRIC Not like Mary to overlook something. Not like her at all...

EDMUND *returns with* MELANIE. *She is wearing her coat and clutches a slim cardboard folder.*

EDMUND *(ushering* MELANIE *in)* Here we are, madam. This way, please.

CEDRIC *(without looking up)* Now, Mary, my dear girl, what on earth can you have overlook– *(seeing* MELANIE*)* Oh. Melanie. It's you...

MELANIE Mr Collison...

CEDRIC What on earth are you doing here, Melanie?

MELANIE *(rapidly spilling it out)* Mr Collison, I'm so sorry, but I urgently need to talk to you...it's extremely urgent... I'm so sorry to be bursting in on you like this. I know it's your wedding anniversary...and I guessed you'd be dining here, like you usually do – I'm so dreadfully sorry. In normal circumstances, I promise, I wouldn't have dreamt of disturbing you, not at all, but I simply had to see you. It's a matter of tremendous importance, Cedric, it really is –

CEDRIC *(calmly)* Melanie... Melanie, my dear. Now slow down. You must slow down, Melanie. Now take it calmly, dear... calmly...

EDMUND *(concerned)* Is everything all right, Mr Collison? You want me to –?

CEDRIC No, everything's fine, Edmund. I can deal with this, it's perfectly all right. I know this lady very well.

EDMUND Only, if she's here under false pretences –?

CEDRIC You can get me another one of these, Edmund. Sit down for a minute, Melanie – Would you like a drink as well, my dear? You seem very flustered...

MELANIE No, thank you, I don't want to drink anything, I just need to talk to you. I have to warn you, you see –

CEDRIC Well, do have something. A glass of water, perhaps...

MELANIE A glass of water, yes, please...a glass of water...

CEDRIC One more vodka and a glass of water, Edmund... Now, for heaven's sake, do sit down, woman...

EDMUND Vodka martini and a glass of water, sir.

CEDRIC Edmund! Do make sure it's plain water. Nothing fancy. This place does have plain bog-standard water, I take it?

EDMUND Indeed it does, sir.

He goes off towards the bar.

MELANIE *(as soon as he goes)* Mr Collison, I have to tell you something quite terrible – I'm here to warn you that something absolutely terrible is going to happen –

CEDRIC Melanie, please. Will you please sit down. I refuse to listen to you until you sit and calm down. Now sit! Sit! Please. Then, I promise I will listen to you. I promise.

MELANIE *sits at the table.*

Deep breaths. Take it slowly, Melanie. Now, what's all this about?

MELANIE You're in terrible danger, Mr Collison. I've come to warn you, you're in the most terrible danger...

CEDRIC What danger is this, Melanie? What makes you think I'm in danger?

MELANIE Because I heard them. Planning to kill you.

CEDRIC *(remaining calm)* Kill me? Who's this planning to kill me, exactly? Who are they?

MELANIE Your wife and – and another person...

CEDRIC Cora? You mean Cora? My wife is planning to kill me?

MELANIE I heard them. Him and her.

CEDRIC Him? Who's him?

MELANIE Her – her lover – I presume he's her lover, anyway. He sounded like her lover...

CEDRIC Cora? Her lover? My wife doesn't have a lover. Who?

MELANIE His name's Freddy. I don't know his full name...she just called him Freddy. Tall, good-looking...athletic. If you like that sort of thing...

CEDRIC Freddy? We don't know anyone called Freddy.

MELANIE Well, your wife certainly does...

CEDRIC *(musing)* Freddy? Freddy? No... *(sudden thought)* Fredericks, perhaps?

MELANIE Frederick! Possibly. That could be him...

CEDRIC Donald Fredericks, he was my late wife's doctor. Heart specialist, retired now. Possibly dead, for all I know...

MELANIE No, this man was young, very young. Younger than she was. Much, much younger.

EDMUND *returns from the bar with another vodka and a tumbler and a jug of iced water.*

CEDRIC Ah, thank you.

MELANIE Thank you very much.

EDMUND Madam. Will the lady be joining you for dinner, sir?

MELANIE *(alarmed)* Oh, no...

CEDRIC Oh, no, no, no! I don't think so. You'll let me know when the rest of them arrive, Edmund, won't you?

EDMUND Of course, sir. Will you be requiring anything else?

CEDRIC No thank you. We'll call if we need you.

EDMUND Thank you, sir.

He goes off in the direction of the bar.

CEDRIC Listen Melanie, I'd love to hear more about this, I can't say I'm not intrigued but I do have a table booked here in just over fifteen minutes' time. I'm expecting my wife and four old and dear friends –

MELANIE – to celebrate your tenth wedding anniversary. I know. Tonight's the night they're planning to do it...

CEDRIC What, over dinner? Here? In the middle of Mayhew's? What on earth are they planning to do? Poison my soup?

MELANIE No, they're planning to push you off a cliff.

CEDRIC Off a cliff? What cliff? Listen, Melanie, this is making no sense at all. You're going to have to start from the beginning. Now you overheard them, you say?

MELANIE Yes.

CEDRIC Plotting to kill me?

MELANIE Yes.

CEDRIC My wife and this mysterious chap, Freddy?

MELANIE I know it all sounds ridiculous telling it like this...

CEDRIC Where did you overhear them, Melanie? Where exactly?

MELANIE In a restaurant.

CEDRIC And where was this restaurant?

MELANIE Oh, it's just my local bistro, I often go there for dinner. It's very close to where I live. In Clapham Junction.

CEDRIC *(faintly incredulous)* Clapham Junction? My wife was eating in a bistro near Clapham Junction?

MELANIE Yes.

CEDRIC With this chap called Freddy?

MELANIE Yes, they were both in disguise.

CEDRIC In disguise? What sort of disguise?

MELANIE She was wearing dark glasses and a headscarf and he had this big ridiculous hat on.

CEDRIC *(swallowing this with difficulty)* All right. They were both in this bistro near Clapham Junction in disguise and where were you, Melanie?

MELANIE *(aware she is losing credibility)* I was – I was in there, too. I was waiting for David.

CEDRIC David? Who's David?

MELANIE My husband, David. He was meeting John at Paddington.

CEDRIC John? Who's John?

MELANIE My son, John. I told you about my son. You must remember John? I used to have his picture on my desk.

CEDRIC Oh, yes, John. The one who looked very like –

MELANIE Like a young George Clooney, yes. He's very handsome, they're often getting mistaken. John's at Oxford. He's reading Law, Physics and Social Psychology. He was travelling down with Sally.

CEDRIC Sally? Who's Sally?

MELANIE His fiancée. She's an arts graduate and a middle-distance athlete.

CEDRIC So you were all in there together, were you? Having a jolly time?

MELANIE No, just me. They didn't turn up.

CEDRIC No? Why's that, do you think, Melanie?

MELANIE We – must have missed each other.

CEDRIC So you were there all on your own, were you? In this bistro?

MELANIE Yes.

CEDRIC Along with my wife and – Freddy? Both in disguise?

MELANIE That's right.

CEDRIC And what about you? Were you in disguise as well, Melanie?

MELANIE No, only them. Only they were in disguise. Why on earth should I need to be in disguise?

CEDRIC *(losing patience, somewhat)* I haven't the faintest idea, Melanie! But then quite frankly, I cannot for the life of me fathom why anyone would need to be in disguise in a bistro in Clapham...

MELANIE *(getting agitated)* You don't believe a word of this, do you? I knew you weren't going to believe me, I knew it...

CEDRIC *(calming her)* No, no, no! Come along, come along. I'm sorry. So. Tell me the rest of it. How did you come to overhear them?

MELANIE *(hesitantly)* Well...

CEDRIC You were at the next table, presumably?

MELANIE No...

CEDRIC Did you overhear them talking at the next table, was that it?

MELANIE *(in a small voice)* No. I was at the same table.

CEDRIC I'm sorry? You're saying, you were at the same table?

MELANIE Yes.

CEDRIC The same table as they were?

MELANIE Yes.

CEDRIC Were you having dinner together, then?

MELANIE No.

CEDRIC So you were sitting at their table whilst they were plotting to murder me? Don't you feel that was a trifle indiscreet of them, Melanie? Particularly when they'd gone to all the trouble to disguise themselves?

MELANIE *starts to cry.*

Melanie...

MELANIE *(shaking her head, weeping)* It all sounds so stupid, now...

CEDRIC *(very gently to her)* Melanie, we've been through all this before, haven't we? Many times, dear. This is the reason you couldn't carry on working for us, wasn't it? – Because of your – the state of your health. You're not at all well, Melanie, are you?

MELANIE I'm not making it up, I promise I'm not. I swear I'm not making it up.

CEDRIC *(placing his hand on hers, gently)* Yes, but you see what about all those other times, Melanie? All those other times in the office? You swore you weren't making any of those up, either, didn't you? And we did have all these problems, you see, didn't we? With these continuous hallucinations of yours? Strange alien creatures in the stationery store. Mysterious beings in the board room. You swore once you saw Jesus working the photocopier. You upset a lot of our staff, you know, Melanie, especially the younger ones. A number of the juniors were terrified to go home on their own after dark, you know...

MELANIE *(gripping his hand impetuously with both of hers)* I do love you so much, Cedric.

CEDRIC *(easing his hand from hers)* Yes, I know you do. And we've talked about that, as well, haven't we? We've talked and talked about it. But it's just not practical, you see, Melanie, is it? We've been through all this before, haven't we? I'm a happily married man and I have a wife whom I love very much –

MELANIE She's not worthy of you, Cedric! She doesn't deserve you! She's a gold-digging little whore and a deceitful harlot –

CEDRIC *(sternly)* Now that's enough, Melanie! That's quite enough of that! She's my wife. I won't have you talking about Cora like that, I really won't! And you're not to write her any more of those letters of yours, either! You know what the judge told you. Any more of that and you could well finish up in prison. Now please, just go home, Melanie! Please!

EDMUND *appears in the entrance.*

EDMUND Excuse me, Mr Collison...

CEDRIC *(somewhat relieved)* Oh, have they arrived?

EDMUND Just Mrs Collison, sir.

CEDRIC Oh, good.

EDMUND She's just in the cloakroom.

CEDRIC Tell her I'm here.

EDMUND I will, sir.

He goes off.

CEDRIC Now, people are starting to arrive, Melanie. You really have to –

MELANIE *(urgently)* After dinner, you're planning to drive back to your cottage, aren't you?

CEDRIC Now, Melanie, please...that's enough, now!

MELANIE Aren't you? Planning to drive there?

CEDRIC Yes, probably, we are, yes.

MELANIE When you get there, she's going to suggest, since it's your tenth anniversary, it would be romantic if you both secretly renewed your marriage vows, just the two of you...

CEDRIC Ah, well, yes, that does sound romantic, I must say...

MELANIE And then she'll suggest that, at midnight, you both walk up to the place where you first proposed to her –

CEDRIC What, up at Craghead Rock?

MELANIE At Craghead Rock, yes! But once you're up there, standing on the edge of the cliff, he'll be hiding in the bushes, waiting for you –

CEDRIC Who will?

MELANIE Freddy. Who do you think? And then she'll – she'll distract you and then he'll push you over... She'll claim it was an accident. Do you see?

CEDRIC Melanie, really! You've seriously lost all touch with reality, dear. You're living in a world entirely of your own –

MELANIE You have to believe me –

CEDRIC This is a complete fabrication. Don't you see? None of it is real, my dear. None of it! Husbands, sons at Oxford, middle-distance-running fiancées! Disguises! Secret plots to murder me – where's it all going to end –?

EDMUND *enters with* **CORA**.

CORA *(as she enters)* Sorry, darling, I got stuck in the most appalling traffic – Piccadilly's horrendous – *(seeing* **MELANIE***)* Oh, for God's sake, it's not you again, is it? I thought we'd got rid of you finally and for ever, Melanie –

MELANIE *(wheeling on* **CORA***)* Yes. That's what you hoped, you whore! You murderous bitch!

CORA *(taken aback)* I beg your pardon!

CEDRIC Melanie!

EDMUND Madam, I really must ask you to moderate –

MELANIE *(confronting* **CORA***)* Well, you're not getting away with it, you conniving witch! You and your toy-boy! You won't get away with it, do you hear?

CORA *(contemptuously)* Get out of my way you batty, demented creature!

She makes to push **MELANIE** *aside.*

MELANIE *responds by grabbing hold of* CORA *and trying to grapple her.*

MELANIE Witch! Witch! Witch!

CEDRIC *(during this)* Now, that's quite enough of that –

EDMUND *(during this)* Ladies! Ladies, please! Ladies!

CORA *(indignantly)* OW! Will you stop that at once, you mad, mad – lunatic!

The fight, such as it is, is brief and sudden. CORA *overpowers* MELANIE *with some ease and pins her to the floor.* MELANIE *flails helplessly and then goes limp.*

EDMUND, *somewhat belatedly, gathers* MELANIE *up and frogmarches her out of the door.*

EDMUND *(as he propels* MELANIE*)* Come along, madam, this way...

MELANIE *(as she goes)* Cedric, I beg you, whatever you do, don't trust her...don't trust her...please...believe me...you have to believe me...

Her voice cuts off as she is apparently deposited in the street outside.

CORA My God! I thought we'd seen the last of her, Mad Melanie! How'd she get in here, for heaven's sake?

CEDRIC She blagged her way in, pretending to be my PA...

CORA Not anymore she's not! No way! How long's she been here?

CEDRIC Oh, about ten minutes.

CORA You poor darling, has she been giving you a hard time? Dreadful woman! All those poisonous letters she wrote to me. She's seriously dangerous...

CEDRIC No, not really, not dangerous. She's a bit sad, really.

CORA Oh, my darling, you work so hard all day and then, on top of it all, you have to put up with that. On our wedding anniversary, as well. What was she after? What did she want?

CEDRIC Oh, well she...she wanted to...no, don't let's even go there. You're right, she's crazy. Crazy woman.

EDMUND *returns.*

Well done! You get rid of her, Edmund?

EDMUND I put her into the street, sir, but she tried to get straight back in again. I've left her with the doorman. We've had to call the police.

CEDRIC Oh, dear. I had hoped we could have avoided that.

EDMUND Your guests have arrived, by the way, sir. They're just checking their coats.

CEDRIC Oh, splendid.

CORA Jolly good! We'll come out and say hallo.

EDMUND *goes.*

CEDRIC Sorry, darling, I didn't ask. You feeling all right? After your little scrap?

CORA Oh, yes, I'm perfectly fine.

CEDRIC Very impressive! Like a female 007. I was most impressed.

CORA Yes, it certainly pays off!

CEDRIC What does?

CORA With my personal trainer? All these keep-fit and combat sessions.

CEDRIC Oh, those! Still sticking at those, are you?

CORA Got to do something, darling, haven't I, while you're out all day? Must say he's very good, is Freddy.

CEDRIC Freddy?

CORA Oh, of course, you've yet to meet Freddy, haven't you? He's really good news... *(moving off, calling)* Hallo, Marjorie! Dennis! So sweet of you both to come...

CEDRIC Freddy? No. I've yet to meet Freddy. *(moving off, calling)* Dennis! You old rogue, how you keeping...?

The lights fade.

Aftermath...

Some twelve hours later. Wednesday morning. An interview room at a police station.

MELANIE *is now seated on one of two chairs at the table, which is now bare.*

She is very subdued and tired, having spent the night in a police cell.

Offstage, the sound of a male voice, still slightly drunk from the night before, shouting in protest. This continues for a while.

MELANIE *(at length, irritably)* Oh, do be quiet, you wretched man! *(shouting)* Shut up! Shut up! Shut up!

(to herself) All night long!

She looks about her miserably.

The sound of the door being unlocked.

After a moment, a **POLICE SERGEANT** *enters.*

SERGE *(calling behind him as he enters)* All right! All right! You just wait your turn! *(cheerfully, to her)* You all right there, then?

MELANIE How much longer do you intend to keep me here? How much longer?

SERGE Up to twenty-four hours, we can hold you, that's the rule –

MELANIE Twenty-four hours! A whole night in that wretched little cell, the size of a postage stamp and now in this poky little room –

SERGE You don't like the accommodation, love, don't book yourself in the first place. Behave yourself and stop disturbing the peace.

The offstage drunk starts shouting again.

MELANIE And will you please do something to quieten that dreadful man, he's been at that all night.

SERGE It's all right, he's going home in a minute.

MELANIE Lucky him!

SERGE Want a cup of something while you're waiting, do you?

MELANIE I might as well I suppose. Yes.

SERGE Please. Yes, *please.*

MELANIE Please.

SERGE Tea or coffee?

MELANIE Coffee. Please.

SERGE It's instant.

MELANIE Oh, God! Then tea. I'll have tea.

SERGE Please.

MELANIE Please.

SERGE One tea, it is! Milk? Sugar?

MELANIE Milk. No Sugar. *Please.*

SERGE Coming up. Don't worry, he'll be here soon. He's on his way.

MELANIE Who's on his way?

SERGE *(making to leave)* The lawyer. He's on his way.

MELANIE I've already said, I don't need a lawyer, I have no need of a lawyer.

SERGE Oh yes you have, my love! You certainly have.

As he opens the door, the offstage drunk resumes his shouting.

(to the drunk, as he goes) All right, I'm coming! Only one pair of hands, haven't I?

He goes.

The sound of the door being locked again.

Offstage, the drunk is heard arguing with the SERGEANT.

MELANIE, *alone again, rises irritably. She paces a little. Suddenly there is silence, as the voices cease.*

The door is unlocked again.

A FEMALE PC *enters.*

PC *(brusquely)* Visitor for you.

She stands aside and CEDRIC *enters anxiously.*

The PC *leaves. The sound of the door being re-locked after her.*

MELANIE Mr Collison...

CEDRIC Hallo, Melanie, I'm so, so sorry about all this. Oh, God, look at you! Locked up in this wretched police station! I'm so sorry this had to happen to you...

MELANIE *(confused)* Cedric, you're still alive! How come you're here –? What's happening –? What are you –?

CEDRIC I've come to get you out of here, Melanie, away from this dreadful place.

MELANIE But I don't understand, what's happening?

CEDRIC I'll explain everything. The first thing to do is to get you out of here. It's all been taken care of. I just need to sort things out with these people, just a bit of paperwork, that's all, then I'll drive you home –

MELANIE You mean, I'm free to go? I thought they were bringing charges? They told me Cora was going to bring charges?

CEDRIC Yes, she was, I persuaded her to drop them. Under the circumstances she's in no fit state, poor darling... It was tragic.

MELANIE Why, what's happened?

CEDRIC She – a very close friend of hers, Freddy Matthews, he
was her personal trainer, you remember? He had the most
terrible accident, last night in the dark, toppled off a cliff,
poor chap. Killed outright. I don't know what the hell he
was doing up there in the middle of the night, all on his
own. Cora's beside herself with grief, poor love.

MELANIE Oh, dear Lord...

CEDRIC Worst thing of all, I think the police actually believe
Cora may have something to do with it. With the chap's
death. Can you credit that? They're actually holding her
for questioning...

MELANIE But I don't understand, how can –?

CEDRIC Listen, Melanie, we can talk later. Not here. Not now.
Certainly not in a bloody police station, I'll explain everything
in due course. The first thing we need to do is to get you out
of here – *(calling)* Officer! Constable! We're finished in here,
thank you! *(to* MELANIE*)* Wait there. Won't be a moment.
I'll be right back.

The sound of the door being unlocked.

The PC *enters. She stands aside to allow* CEDRIC *to pass.*

We're all done here, thank you, Constable.

PC Sir.

CEDRIC *exits, blowing* MELANIE *a kiss.*

(to MELANIE*)* Wait there, you.

The PC *goes out.*

Sound of the door being relocked.

MELANIE, *on her own, is filled with mixed emotions:
amazement, shock and happiness. This has all happened
so quickly.*

MELANIE *(as the realisation dawns on her)* Oh! Oh, my goodness! Oh, how wonderful! How simply wonderful...

She stands, radiant with happiness.

The sound of the door being unlocked.

(turning to the door, expectantly) Cedric –?

The SERGEANT *enters with a cup of tea, with a wrapped biscuit in the saucer.*

The sound of the drunk again complaining in the background.

SERGE *(calling behind him)* I said, wait! I'm just bringing this lady her cup of tea first! You wait! *(to himself)* Some people! Must think we're running a bloody hotel, don't they? *(to* MELANIE*)* Here we are, my love. Not too strong. Milk, no sugar. Brought you a biccy as well. There.

MELANIE Thank you, that's very kind. But I don't think I'll be needing the tea, after all.

SERGE No?

MELANIE Not now that I'll be leaving.

SERGE Leaving? Where you going?

MELANIE The gentleman who just came in will be driving me home shortly. As soon as he's seen to the necessary paperwork...

SERGE What gentleman?

MELANIE Cedric – Mr Collison. The man who's just been in to see me.

The SERGEANT *looks blank.*

With the police constable. The female police constable.

SERGE Female police constable? We certainly don't have one of them. Apart from Emily. But she's off today. She's not due back till tomorrow. Sooner the better.

We're that short-staffed. Coping all on my own here, aren't I? Lawyer won't be long, he's apparently stuck in traffic!

The drunk shouts again.

The SERGEANT *goes out.*

(as he goes) Just hark at him, will you? *(calling)* All right! Here I come!

The sound of the door being relocked.

MELANIE *stands deflated and miserable.*

MELANIE *(to herself)* Not due back till tomorrow? Tomorrow? *(suddenly realising the implications of this)* Tomorrow. Oh God, it's happening to me again... It's all happening again...

As she stands there apprehensively, the lights fade to:

Blackout.

End of Play

FURNITURE AND PROPS

Premonitions

Table

Basic glassware and crockery

Three mobile phones (Melanie, Cora, Freddy)

Two handbags (Melanie, Cora)

Watch

Headscarf

Dark glasses

Jug of iced tap water

Large gin and tonic

Cap

Tray

Two Scotch and sodas

Bill in bill folder

Water jug refill

Repercussions

Table

Coaster

Fancy cocktail

Three vodka martinis

Mobile phone (Cedric)

Bowl of nuts

Coat (Melanie)

Slim cardboard folder

Tumbler

Jug of water

Aftermath...

Table

Two chairs

Cup of tea with saucer

Biscuit

SOUND EFFECTS

Premonitions

Repercussions

Aftermath...

LIGHTING CUES

Premonitions

Repercussions

Aftermath...

ABOUT THE AUTHOR

Alan Ayckbourn has worked in theatre as a playwright and director for over fifty years, rarely if ever tempted by television or film, which perhaps explains why he continues to be so prolific. To date he has written more than eighty plays, many one-act plays and a large amount of work for the younger audience. His work has been translated into over thirty-five languages, is performed on stage and television throughout the world and has won countless awards.

Major successes include: *Relatively Speaking, How the Other Half Loves, Absurd Person Singular, Bedroom Farce, A Chorus of Disapproval,* and *The Norman Conquests.* In recent years, there have been revivals of *Season's Greetings* and *A Small Family Business* at the National Theatre; in the West End *Absent Friends, A Chorus of Disapproval, Relatively Speaking* and *How the Other Half Loves*; and at Chichester Festival Theatre, major revivals of *Way Upstream* in 2015 and *The Norman Conquests* in 2017. 2019 also saw the publication of his first work of prose fiction, *The Divide.*

Artistic director of the Stephen Joseph Theatre from 1972–2009, where almost all his plays have been first staged, he continues to direct his latest new work there. He was honoured to be appointed the SJT's first Director Emeritus during 2018. He has been inducted into the American Theater Hall of Fame, received the 2010 Critics' Circle Award for Services to the Arts and became the first British playwright to receive both Olivier and Tony Special Lifetime Achievement Awards. He was knighted in 1997 for services to the theatre.

Farcicals

FlatSpin

GamePlan

Gizmo

Haunting Julia

Henceforward...

Hero's Welcome

House & Garden

How the Other Half Loves

If I Were You

Improbable Fiction

Intimate Exchanges, Volume I

Intimate Exchanges, Volume II

It Could Be Any One of Us

Joking Apart

Just Between Ourselves

Life and Beth

Life of Riley

Living Together

Man of the Moment

Me, Myself and I

Lightning Source UK Ltd.
Milton Keynes UK
UKHW022131260220
359385UK00006B/288